Finnegan's Way

Finnegan's Way:

The Secret Power
of Doing Things Badly

By Charles Kelly

ASCLEPIAN IMPRINTS LTD.

A NOTE TO THE READER:

The following story is a fable. None of it is true. Furthermore, the author's credentials are minimal. Charles Kelly does not hold a Ph.D. degree in psychology from Yale University (1970) or a Masters' in Business Administration degree from Harvard University (1973). People do not pay him consulting fees amounting to hundreds of thousands of dollars a year to help them solve personal and business problems. He is merely a former reporter for *The Arizona Republic* who has published two novels, *Pay Here* and *Grace Humiston and the Vanishing*, one biography, *Gunshots in Another Room: The Forgotten Life of Dan J. Marlowe*, and one short story, "The Eighth Deadly Sin," in the collection *Phoenix Noir* published by Akashic Press. He has written enough unpublished novels and stories to fill up a basement, if he had a basement. His record of failure is impressive. No, stunning.

"To illustrate the power of these principles, I wrote *Finnegan's Way* as badly as possible, though not as badly as James Joyce wrote *Finnegans Wake*." (Charles Kelly)

"I make nothing of it whatever."
(Ezra Pound, speaking of *Finnegans Wake*)

"(*Finnegans Wake*) is the pinnacle of literary achievement in the history of civilization itself." (Will Miller)

TABLE OF CONTENTS

CHAPTER 1

Encountering Finnegan

THE IMPORTANCE OF DOING THINGS BADLY would never have come home to me if I hadn't encountered Finnegan one day at a Starbucks coffee shop in Scottsdale, Arizona.

Let me set the scene for you. Outside, it was a bright day in late October, and the air was pungent with the odors of saguaro, paloverde and creosote bush. Arizona was easing toward another delightful winter, and the lean man sipping a double espresso at a corner table seemed to be enjoying himself immensely, though all he was doing was poring over a slim volume bound in rich cloth.

He cut a fine figure. His suit—which obviously came from Savile Row—was sumptuous white linen. His white shirt was open-collared. His cap-toed shoes were polished to a mahogany gloss.

As I noted those details and edged into the coffee line, a distraught-looking woman entered, spied him and rushed up to his table. He laid down his book, smiled and formally extended a hand. Lawyer and client, or doctor and patient, I thought, as the orders for lattes and espressos and decaf cappuccinos began to erupt around me.

The coffee server had caught me eyeing the man in the corner, and when I called for a tall coffee-of-the-day, the Colombia Narino, he arched an eyebrow and informed me, "That's Finnegan."

"Really?" I replied.

"Really," said the server, after he had turned to call out my order to the coffee-prep man. "Big CEO at one time, in England, I think. Made a pile. Now he helps people all the time." He nodded significantly. "Tells them to mess up."

Surely, my ears had tricked me. That couldn't be what he'd really said. But I didn't have time to ask him to clarify. Just then my coffee arrived and the line behind me was making a push.

I might not have bothered to ask him anyway, because at the time I had plenty of other things to worry about. I was running a small publishing operation in downtown Phoenix, specializing in cookbooks, local travel guides, and accounts of Arizona history, and it looked like I was running it into the ground.

Nothing was working. My freelancers were turning in junk, my secretaries were slow in getting out the contracts to the printer, my marketing people weren't hitting up enough bookstores and other outlets. I was sinking, slowly but surely. Bankruptcy was tugging at my sleeve. The fact was, I shouldn't have been ordering coffee at all, because it was just going to attack my insides with another wave of acid. I already had an ulcer on the way.

As I turned and made for the door, I felt a twinge of desperation. Maybe I, too, needed some advice from the mysterious Finnegan. I was willing to try anything.

I hesitated, to see if I might be able to catch him for a few moments. But he was deeply involved with the woman's problems, and the few snatches of conversation I heard didn't give me much confidence in his abilities as an advisor. In fact, they made me question his sanity.

The woman was relatively young, about 40 or so. Her hair was expensively cut, but matted by nervous perspiration, and too many pounds swelled the hips of her fashionable black pants. It was clear, too, that she was disorganized.

She fished around in her turquoise-beaded purse before coming up with documents to show Finnegan. I caught the words "divorce," "anti-depressants," and "co-dependent," shorthand for personal problems endemic to a New Frontier place like Scottsdale.

What wisdom would Finnegan impart? Perhaps if I caught some flavor of it, I would know whether he might offer me hope. I didn't want to stand there hovering, but the answer wasn't long in coming.

Strangely, Finnegan tapped his titanium-rimmed

eyeglasses and looked at me with his long-seeing eyes as he launched into his prescription for the woman's problems.

"You are in a depressing quandary," he told her. "But it will be easy to come out in fine shape. First of all, though, you have to make a vow to me. If I tell you to do something, you must do it in the worst possible way."

The worst possible way? I groaned. With all I was going through, I didn't need this kind of disappointment, too. I abandoned my eavesdropping and slammed through the door, so abruptly that I spilled coffee down the front of my suit. In disgust, I pitched the rest of the cup in a trash barrel and kept going.

I was going to have to face the day with sloppy clothes, lousy prospects, and the words of a nut case ringing in my ears. Do things "in the worst possible way." Excellent. Right. Wonderful. Thanks, Finnegan. I was doing that already. So much for your advice. I could easily be stupid on my own.

As I turned the key in my Toyota Avalon, I was still wondering about what the coffee server had said, though I didn't have time to puzzle it out. I supposed this was just one more of the mysteries of Scottsdale.

How had someone like Finnegan gotten a reputation for helping people? How had he made so much money running a business? How could he possibly have been a successful CEO?

CHAPTER 2

Do It Badly,
Just Horribly

WHEN I STAGGERED INTO THE STARBUCKS again a week later, events at work had taken a terrible turn. My heart was going like a jackhammer, and I barely registered the presence of Finnegan at his corner table.

I had entered automatically, my mind searching for diversion. The last thing I needed was caffeine. That would throw me into a full-blown panic attack. But a decaf latte might at least calm me down.

I was standing there feeling chills surging up and down my arms and legs when I heard a voice both hearty and warm. Finnegan.

"Excuse me," he was saying, "but you are looking quite pale. Perhaps you should sit for a bit and let the Green Willies roll away."

I made my way to his table and fell into a chair. Of course there was no table service, but he beckoned briskly with his hand, and a customer detached himself from the line and rushed over with a cup of cold water. I drained it and sagged back, closed my eyes.

When I opened them, Finnegan had slipped the slim volume he had been reading into his pocket. And he was examining my face, his eyes curious.

"Business problems or personal?" he asked.

"Business," I murmured, and saw him smile broadly.

"Oh, well, then!" he exclaimed, as if I had just announced that I had a hangnail.

My water cup had been refilled, and I emptied it again, regarding him bitterly. "So business difficulties are simple, are they?" I said. "I guess you've never faced bankruptcy."

He leaned back genially, his eyebrows quirking.

"On the contrary," he said. "In fact, I've faced *down* bankruptcy. Not once, but many times."

Hmmph. Probably just idle boasting.

"You've been in business, I'm told," I said. "What businesses?"

"Oh, many businesses," he replied. "A delivery service, retail sales, the restaurant business, consulting, publishing. Among others."

"Publishing," I said. "That happens to be my business. I run a small operation, and I've got several big problems." I added, ironically, "Perhaps you can help."

He smiled charmingly. "Oh, I'm sure I can."

All right. We would see about that. I explained one of my thorniest difficulties. I was having trouble with the quality control on my cookbooks.

6

To save money, I'd gone from a process of using sewn signatures to secure the pages in perfect-bound volumes to gluing in the pages. The pages kept coming loose, and my customers were furious.

I put it to Finnegan: What instructions could I give to the printer so that I could produce higher-quality books?

Finnegan's smile widened and grew wiser.

"You know," he said, "I haven't the faintest idea."

Just as I suspected.

"What?" I replied incredulously. "You say you were in publishing? And you can't help me? Did you make any money?"

"Oh, millions," Finnegan said, unfazed. "Actually, millions and millions, my accountants tell me."

I said acidly, "And how did you manage to do that? You don't seem to know anything about a process that is basic to publishing."

"I don't," he admitted. "But someone does. Probably someone who works for you. Or the printer himself. Tell me, are you trying to do the best you can in solving this problem?"

"Of course I am! I have the highest standards, and I communicate them to my workers and my suppliers. I tell them in no uncertain terms that they had better do the best they can or get lost."

Finnegan nodded sympathetically. "Just as I thought. You are going about things in exactly the wrong way."

I was about ready to explode. "How can I be doing

the wrong thing when I demand that they do things well?"

"It is very simple," Finnegan said, placing his right pointer finger on the table as if marking a page in a book. "You should be telling them to do things badly."

My belly tightened. Now it was all coming back to me.

"Oh," I said. "I get it. I'm just like that woman who asked you for advice the other day. Your brilliant idea is that I should do things in the worst way possible."

"No, no," he replied benignly. "Hers was an extreme case. But yours is quite easy. If you and your workers do things badly, just horribly, that should be sufficient."

"What?" I said. "You are telling me to accept failure?"

"Of course not," replied Finnegan. "Doing badly is not failure. It is a way of *avoiding* failure, of outfoxing the forces that *bring on* failure."

By now I was so confused and worried and weary, that I couldn't find it in myself to be angry any more. I simply shook my head and said, "I don't understand."

He reached across the table and patted my hand. "Soon, you will."

Finnegan leaned back. "Tell me," he said, "When you demand the best of your workers, how does that work out?"

I considered. "Well," I said, "Some of them, the really good ones, do very well. They do just what I tell them to do. The others, well, you know, there aren't a lot of good workers around. I just get rid of the bad ones and get some more."

"It's so frustrating, isn't it?" said Finnegan. "I suppose you've done your best to improve things by posting 'mission statements' in your workers' cubicles, telling them to clean up their desks and rationing the number of Form X's and batteries they use. Am I correct?"

"Well. . .yes," I said. "I've done something like that."

"Then, a couple of weeks later, things start to get back to normal. Oh, maybe you chastise someone for having a dirty coffee cup or using an extra battery, but no-one really seems to care."

"That's true," I said. "It's terrible. What exactly is going on there?"

"What is going on there is good sense re-asserting itself," said Finnegan. "This is wisdom finding its own level. This is the system deciding how much bad personal behavior it will tolerate. And, usually, it will tolerate a lot."

"Why, that's nonsense!" I said. "It's just rebellion. And it's all caused by those bad workers."

"Yes," nodded Finnegan. "Those bad workers. Those bad, bad workers." He thought about that for a moment. "But your good workers do just what you tell them. Do they continue to do that, year after year?"

"You bet they do," I said, regaining a bit of enthusiasm. "It's remarkable how they can stick to my program. That shows real quality."

"Does it now?" said Finnegan. "And are they happy?"

"I'm not one of these coddling managers who cares

9

all that much if my workers are happy," I shot back. "They are there to do a job, and by golly, I expect them to do it."

"It sounds like they aren't doing the job very well, though," he pointed out. "Since you are facing bankruptcy."

I felt instantly deflated. "Well, no," I said. "I suppose they aren't."

"And you aren't doing a very good job as a manager," he continued.

"No," I sighed. "I suppose I'm not."

His face glowed. "Then perhaps you are ready for my way."

I shrugged. I genuinely didn't see any way out.

"I suppose I could try it," I said. "However crazy it is, what have I got to lose?"

"Exactly," said Finnegan.

CHAPTER 3

Finnegan's Way

"IT'S REMARKABLE," I WAS TELLING FINNEGAN cautiously several days later. "I'm not saying that there has been a complete turnaround, but things are definitely showing signs of improvement."

He bent forward, pressing his palms together.

"Tell me about it."

"Well," I said, "I had some reservations about your method, but in the end, I did as you said. After we talked, I went directly to work and called a meeting of my employees. All of them."

"You say, 'all of them.' Was there a time in the past when you would not have summoned all of them?"

"Oh, yes," I replied. "My normal method would be to just call in the good ones, the leaders, the ones who carry out my program as I have laid it down. After all, why bother with the ones who aren't doing well? But you told me to call them all together, and that's what I did."

"And what exactly did you tell them?"

"I told them, first of all, that we were facing a business disaster, and that I didn't know what to do—"

Finnegan was watching me keenly. "And did they believe you?"

"They did. After all, it was the absolute truth...*is* the absolute truth...and I have been feeling so rotten about it that I'm sure that showed in my face."

"Excellent."

"Then I told them we had some time to play with before the final blow fell, since we are going into a bankruptcy reorganization. In the short run, we'd all continue to have jobs. And while we all still did have jobs—"

I paused. This part had been difficult for me while I was doing it, and it was difficult for me to describe it. It just seemed such a crazy thing to do. But Finnegan was giving me an encouraging look.

"—I told them while we all still had jobs, I wanted them to do those jobs badly. Everyone still had to come to work, and they still had to *do* their jobs—no long sessions playing video games on their computers, for instance, though if they wanted to do some of that, that was all right, too. But their main focus should be on doing their jobs *badly*."

Finnegan seemed ecstatic. "*Focus*," he exclaimed. "I like that word!"

I was eager to continue. "They were very puzzled. I could see that. They were looking at each other, and some were shaking their heads. But, the funny thing is, within seconds, some of them seemed to be nodding as if they understood."

"Did they now?" Finnegan asked. "And which ones were nodding their heads?"

"Well," I said hesitantly. "To tell the truth, it was the bad workers, the ones who had never been very good at carrying out my program."

"Oh yes," Finnegan said, as if making a mental note. "The bad workers. The ones that didn't go along with the program that had led you to the point of business disaster."

"Yes," I said. He was, after all, merely stating a fact. "And. . .that was it. I went back to my office, put my feet up on my desk, said to hell with the rest of my schedule and began to try to figure out how *I* could do things badly. After all, we were all in this together, and I wanted to try your methods myself. First of all, I wanted to see if they would work. Second, I wanted to see if I could understand them."

Finnegan clapped a hand on the table enthusiastically. "You know, I knew immediately when I laid eyes on you that you would be an apt pupil. I said to myself, 'If ever there was a man capable of bad work, that one is!'"

I felt strangely humble. "Why, thank you very much," I replied.

I basked in his praise for a moment, then came to with a start.

"But let me tell you what happened next," I said. "For a couple of days, my workers seemed a bit at sea, as if they didn't really know what to do. But as time went on, I noticed that they were relaxing more and more—the bad ones, in particular—and becoming more playful. Let me give you an example. We have a very rigid way of answering customers who call to order cookbooks. I started this system to make sure we were always polite and that things got done just so. It was something I learned in the Marines. . ."

"A magnificent organization!" interjected Finnegan. "Of course, they always *kill* their customers."

"Yes, I suppose they do," I said, "but let me tell you what happened. I caught one of the order-takers, a sloppily dressed young man, joking around on the phone with a customer, taking much longer to fill the order than we usually do. I almost chastised him, but then I remembered he was supposed to be doing things badly, and kept my silence. Well, he kept joking and chatting with the customer, and in the end, he took a larger order than usual! I thought perhaps this was a fluke, but I noticed several of the other order-takers were following his lead, and at the end of the day, orders for cookbooks had risen!"

"Humanity beats conformity," Finnegan said, almost to himself.

I barely heard him, though, because I was continuing excitedly, "And that wasn't all. I caught one of my staff writers, a woman who has no technical knowledge at all, goofing off and ignoring an article she was supposed to be writing. Instead, she was doodling something on a sheet of paper, some technical drawing with lines and numbers."

"Did you speak to her about it?"

"I did!" I replied. "You would have been proud of me. I gave her a huge smile and said, 'You are doing badly. Good for you!'"

Finnegan clapped his hands. "Good for *you*!" he replied. "Without even any specific instruction, you have grasped another of my principles: Do things badly *with enthusiasm*!"

"That's an excellent idea, even if I say so myself," I countered, laughing. "Now, what do you think she was doing?"

Finnegan leaned back meditatively. "Well, I would say she was trying to do something she'd never done before because she hadn't been encouraged."

"That's right!" I said. "She was trying to solve our problem of having pages fall out of our books."

"Excellent!" Finnegan enthused. "But let's review. What exactly has changed in your workplace?"

I thought about it. "Well, people have eased up, especially the workers that I thought were poor workers. They are trying new things, new approaches," I said cautiously.

"What about your good workers?"

"Well, they are having a harder time accepting change, I think. They seemed more puzzled than the bad workers by the idea that they should do things badly." I looked at him. "Why is that?"

"It's quite simple," said Finnegan. "Like many bosses, you think workers are 'good' if they do what you tell them, even if you are forcing them to take a mediocre approach. Day in and day out, they follow the program, never thinking for themselves." He shook his head. "That is not good. When conditions change, the businesses they work for fail, and they are thrown out of work, wondering what happened. Furthermore, they have a hard time finding work in other fields—because they are so used to being told what to do, they don't trust their own ability to explore."

I was trying to follow this. "And why are the bad workers more adaptable?"

"Again, simple," replied Finnegan. "People who do rotten work often do so because they don't like the boss and think they are getting away with something. They can actually be quite inventive in thinking up reasons why they didn't come to work on time, or didn't finish that job on deadline, or left parts of it out. Their poor performance is a *creative* endeavor."

He paused to make his point. "But they carry out that endeavor only to get back at the boss for being an idiot. If you give them permission to do things badly, their motivation to perform poorly goes away. Especially if you show them, as you did, that the business will go down, and take them with it, if they don't exercise all their skills. When that happens, their natural drive to do things well takes over."

He rapped a knuckle on the table, as if to illustrate

the vigor of that natural drive.

"Being told they can do badly has taken the pressure off them. Now, in this freed-up atmosphere, the creativity they spent on undermining you they now spend on doing an excellent job. They have a stake in what they are doing, and perform outstandingly!"

I was trying to absorb all this, but at the same time, something was nagging at my memory. "You said something right after I told you that my order-takers were no longer behaving like Marines," I said. "What was that?"

Finnegan smiled and repeated what he had said.

CHAPTER 4

Humanity Beats Conformity

"HUMANITY BEATS CONFORMITY," Finnegan said.

"That certainly has a ring to it," I replied, "and I think I get what it means in one way. That you shouldn't do things robotically, time after time. But I sense that it means more than that."

Finnegan, for the first time today, savored his Ethiopia Sidamo—black, no cream or sugar—and set the cup down very carefully, as if its placement on the table were of great significance.

"You are entirely right," he said. "In fact, *Humanity beats conformity* is the key to the success of doing things badly. It applies to both the psychology and the practicality of the matter."

I, too, had a drink of coffee. I was also enjoying the Ethiopia Sidamo, black, no cream or sugar. It seemed that as I was falling more and more under Finnegan's influence, I was beginning to share his tastes.

"When you refer to the psychology of the matter,

what do you mean?" I asked.

"Simply this," replied Finnegan. "Often when we are young, or starting out in a field of endeavor, people tell us we are doing things badly. Now, this is undoubtedly true. In fact, hardly anyone who tries something new does well from the very start. But the message we get is that doing badly is a *negative* thing. People belittle us, criticize us unduly, bring us down. Suddenly, we go from having fun and doing things badly—and making progress here and there—to doing the very safe things that we find we do pretty well from the starting gun."

He propped his chin on the "Y" between his right thumb and forefinger, as if bracing himself to consider things more deeply.

"And the really damaging thing is that we are being led along a pathway that the person in charge believes is correct. '*Do it the way I did it. Don't take chances. Play the percentages.*'"

Finnegan reflected. "There was a time when that worked reasonably well, when you could expect to work all your life for the same company, plugging away at something you were reasonably competent at, even if you hated it." He sighed. "Now, that's all gone. Anyone who doesn't take risks in today's economy is in big trouble."

"And taking risks means doing things badly?"

"Indeed it does. In an industrial economy, there may well be 'one best way' to do many tasks: shoveling coal, inserting a part in an automobile, laying bricks. The efficiency expert, Frederick Winslow Taylor, was the prophet of that approach. But in an economy based on service and information, the human factor takes over to a remarkable degree. Each human being may accomplish things in his or her own special way. But finding that special way often means stumbling along for a period of time."

"Explain."

Finnegan took my denseness with good grace.

"Doing things badly is a method of *exploration*, and it can have surprisingly powerful results," he said. "A writer often finds the best way to write a story by just jumping in and writing whatever comes to mind, letting all the ideas and scenes and bits of dialogue flow across the page. If she finds she's on the wrong track, fine. She stops, takes a deep breath, and starts all over from the beginning. Now she knows she is on the right track, because she has a powerful sense of the *wrong* way to go."

"I don't quite understand," I said.

"Think of it this way," said Finnegan, "You are traveling through a forest and you have two paths you can choose. It happens that you choose the wrong path. You can start along that path and poke along, worrying, wandering a little way off, then coming back to the main way, never really sure if your direction is correct. Or you can rush boldly along that path—doing the wrong thing with all your energy—until the landmarks show you clearly that you are traveling the

21

wrong way. Then you can return to your starting point and strike out with confidence on the correct path."

I sipped coffee and thought about this. "That's a very clear metaphor," I said. "But how does it apply to doing a job?"

Finnegan thought for a moment. "Well, I can tell you of one very clear instance in which it applied to a job. When I was a young man, working for a large international concern, I was stationed in New York City. Some of my friends and I used to like to spend Friday nights drinking at an Irish pub a few blocks from Little Italy. Well, one night after we had imbibed a bit too much, we were very hungry. So we wandered a few blocks and found a small pizza establishment that had only one employee, an elderly Italian man who spoke English very badly."

"Strange," I said. "I never would have taken you for a drinking man."

Finnegan was patient. "This is when I was quite young, as I told you. It is a time of life when one naturally gravitates toward doing things badly."

"Ah, yes," I said. "But you were telling me about Italian food."

"Actually, I was telling you about an elderly Italian man. As it turned out, he did everything at the pizza place: cleaned it, took the orders, and cooked the food."

"Let me guess," I interjected. "He cooked food badly."

"No, actually, he took orders badly," replied Finnegan. "The menu was rich and complex, but it was something of a trap. One of us ordered linguine carbonara, another lasagna, still another pizza with pepperoni, anchovies and green peppers. I asked for spaghetti with meat sauce."

"You mean, he couldn't keep track of all that?"

Finnegan assumed a meditative look. "You know, he seemed to be taking it all down meticulously. But when the order arrived, all he served us was plain cheese pizza and green salad with Italian dressing."

"I suppose you complained bitterly."

"We did indeed," said Finnegan. "But his English suddenly got even worse, and he seemed not to understand us at all."

"I hate bad service. The only way to deal with it is to refuse to pay and walk out. I suppose that's what you did."

"Well, we would have," Finnegan said, "but we were ferociously hungry, and drunk enough not to take ourselves too seriously. Actually, after a few vain protests, we tucked right into the food and devoured it all."

"And it was—?"

"Delicious!" exclaimed Finnegan. I could almost see his mouth watering at the memory. "The pizza had the lightest, flakiest crust, with just a hint of firmness. The tomato sauce was spiced with a blend of flavorings I have never encountered anywhere else. The mix of cheeses was delightful, and the cheeses themselves appeared to be of the highest quality. The salad was crisp and icy, and the dressing carried the tang of lively, unusual herbs."

"Well, you were lucky that the dishes he selected turned out to be good ones."

Finnegan put a finger to his lips. "I don't believe there was any luck involved. I always surmised that our bad order-taker was also bad, or at least mediocre, at preparing the other dishes on the menu. So he simply selected what he did best. Then he did it every day, for every customer, no matter what they ordered."

I nodded. "Instead of doing what everyone else did, he played to his own strengths, and did something unique."

Finnegan was nodding, too.

"Exactly. Humanity beats conformity."

CHAPTER 5

Perfection
is a Pitfall

ONE MORNING WHEN I MADE MY usual Starbucks run, I passed a woman on the way out I believed I recognized. Rather pretty, carrying herself with an attractive sort of confidence.

Though I was almost certain she was not a regular at the shop, I thought I had seen her there. Once I settled down with Finnegan, I asked about her, and he made the connection for me.

"That's the woman who was asking me for advice the first time I saw you, a few weeks ago," he said. "I recall you hanging back while I spoke to her, then leaving without approaching me. I had a feeling, though, that you would approach me at some point."

"I recall her now." I said. "Except she looks much different. Less frantic, more relaxed, even better put together. She seems to have lost some weight, and she walks as if she knows where she's going."

"I am not disputing you on those points," Finnegan

said. "In fact, you are seconding my own observations."

I was listening, but carefully watching, too. I had begun to examine everything about him quite closely.

When I entered, he had been reading the slim volume I had first seen him holding. Now, making no particular effort to conceal the book, he slipped it into a side pocket of his coat. Preparing to do so, he inadvertently gave me a full view of its cover.

The title was right there in front of my eyes—even so, for some reason I couldn't read it. The phenomenon puzzled me, but I quickly forgot it. Finnegan was speaking again, in a mildly mesmerizing way.

Once again, I was drawn into the flow of his conversation.

"Like all my clients," he was saying, "the woman has given me permission to speak in general about her problems, and her success in overcoming them. So I don't hesitate to tell you that she is making exciting progress."

"Progress in her personal life, as opposed to business?" I said. "So Finnegan's Way works there, too?"

Finnegan modestly inclined his head, as if the answer should have been obvious.

"Finnegan's Way, as you put it, is an approach to life itself, not to business alone, so of course it works in personal endeavors."

"And how has this lady applied it?"

"Very simply," he replied. "By avoiding perfection."

I shifted uncomfortably in my seat. "Isn't that a little too basic? It would seem that avoiding perfection would be very easy."

Finnegan took a drink of coffee as he ruminated.

"Failing to be perfect is easy, that is true," he said. "But that is not what I am talking about. I'm referring to consciously avoiding perfection. This woman is on the point of divorce because perfection has become her goal in many areas. She wants to be the perfect wife, have the perfect body, have the perfect relationship with her husband."

I rolled this around in my mind, recalling the woman as I had first seen her.

"That puzzles me," I said. "As I recall, when that woman first consulted you she was overweight and nervous and she seemed quite disorganized. Not what I would call someone who was obsessed with perfection."

"Not true," said Finnegan, waggling a finger. "That was exactly the case with her. She was so obsessed with perfection that she had given up. Her life had become chaotic, she was fighting with her husband all the time, and she had let everything go: her body and her life."

He sighed. "It is a very common situation, unfortunately. Perfection is a pitfall. When one won't settle for half-measures, one quickly gets discouraged and abandons all hope." He lifted his chin. "Have you ever heard the expression, 'The perfect drives out the good?' Well, that is exactly what was happening with this woman."

I thought about this. "So you simply told her to abandon her high standards?"

Finnegan's face glowed.

"Yes I did! In fact, I told her to abandon all standards, and to immediately begin performing in a 'whatever' way. At first, you may recall, I told her to perform in the worst possible way. I did so to force her to focus intensely on her actions. But very quickly I eased up the regime so she was merely performing badly."

He paused and held up a cautioning hand. "Note, however: I instructed her to *perform*. No more sitting around. Here is what I advised:

"To deal with her lack of organization, I told her to jot down a list of things she had to do each day, but not to worry if she forgot something or failed to carry out items on her list.

"To deal with her husband, who has been having an affair, I told her to simply carry on with him as pleasantly as possible.

"To deal with her physical fitness, I told her pick a simple exercise—she chose sit-ups—and to do ten repetitions each morning, badly."

Despite my enthusiasm for Finnegan and his regimen, or lack of it, I felt dubious.

I lifted an eyebrow. "And this has solved all her problems?"

Finnegan laughed uproariously, so much that his shoulders shook.

"Of course it has not solved all her problems!" he

exclaimed. "My Way is a *way*, it is not an instant solution. Everyone wants an instant solution today. Such a solution does not exist! Even you are tempted by the idea that it does. I held my tongue the other day when you said you could see signs of improvement in your workers but not 'a complete turnaround.' You will not see an instant turnaround in them, and this woman will not see it in her life. But she, too, is seeing signs of improvement."

"Specifically, what?"

Finnegan ticked off the changes on his fingers.

"One, she has begun making lists, the absolute best way to get organized. Two, she is thinking about living pleasantly, which has removed her from the emotional turmoil she was having over her husband's affair. Third, her regular exercise is lifting her depression and making her physically more fit."

"But aren't these very minor changes?"

Instead of looking frustrated or annoyed, Finnegan leaned forward as if to engage this point.

"Minor changes, yes, except they have the advantage of being done *badly*. Because they are done badly, and there is no inner voice demanding that they be done well, her daily actions are quickly becoming habits. Good habits. She is converting from bad habits such as doing things in a slapdash way, fighting with her husband, lounging around."

Finnegan raised his hands and cupped them, as if to embrace the woman's new situation. "Her new habits are developing slowly, gradually, easily. As they do, she is going from doing nothing about her problems—or worse, sitting around obsessing about them—to doing little things to change. She is not experiencing a wrenching change of gears, but a smooth, almost effortless shift. Before long, the force of habit will grow more and more powerful. Good instincts will be flowing through her. Subconsciously, she will be improving all the time."

I took all this in, meditating on what he had said.

"I see what you mean. But all that is a bit complex for me." I smiled. "Knowing you, I'm sure you can reduce what you have just said to a simple principle."

It was Finnegan's turn to smile.

"You are getting to know me very well," he said. "Of course this is the expression of a principle, and here it is:

"The problem is not that people don't perform *well*. It is that they don't *perform*."

CHAPTER 6

Help Others Do Things Badly

AS TIME WENT ON, I WAS beginning more and more to believe that the methods Finnegan suggested were workable and effective, and I wanted to explore them in detail. He was always open to this.

Indeed, he was open to anything. He offered his advice readily to anyone who asked for it, and never asked to be paid. Even those who took his suggestions and went away without thanking him—and occasionally someone did—went away with his blessing.

"What are *you* getting out of this?" I asked him one day. "What are you getting out of counseling people, of directing them to the good by pointing them down the path of doing things badly?"

By this time, he seemed to enjoy not only my efforts to extract all his knowledge, but also my skepticism about how and why his suggestions worked. I knew that normally people did not challenge him, but simply accepted him as a wise man.

While he seemed perfectly comfortable with this role, I knew he must enjoy the intellectual stimulation of someone who tried to probe the weak points of his advice, or who—at least—questioned its underpinnings. Now I was stepping up my challenge, questioning not only the advice but his motive in providing it.

"What am I getting out of this?" he responded with an impish smile. "I'm a little dismayed at your question. Correct me if I'm wrong, but it seems to imply criticism. Do you think I'm operating badly as an advice enterprise? Are you shocked that I'm handing out advice for free, improving the lives of people, but never making a dollar?"

Now he had me on the defensive.

"No," I replied. "I don't criticize you for not making a profit, although you apparently have devoted a great deal of your life to that. But we all have motives for the way we lead our lives, we all expect some sort of reward for our actions—monetary, psychological or spiritual—and I can't see where you are being rewarded."

"Actually, that is a good question." He smiled. "You always ask such good questions. It's a remarkable gift."

"Now you are trying to reward me," I said, "Rather than answering the question."

He chuckled gently. "And you are so observant!"

Then he inserted his thumbs behind the lapels of his coat and began to drum his fingertips on his chest, bending his head in an attitude of contemplation.

"I apologize," he said at last. "I have been having a

32

bit of fun with you, I suppose. But then, fun is a motive, too, along with all the grandiose ones you have just listed. Yes, I have made a great deal of money in my life, and I suppose that from time to time, I have dwelled on whether I was also going to obtain psychological or spiritual satisfaction. But life is not nearly so clear-cut as you present it. You seem to think that every human endeavor consists of setting a goal, constantly moving towards it, weighing what we will get when we reach it."

He sighed a bit and cocked his head toward the ceiling as his fingertips continued to beat in rhythm.

"That is not the way most people operate, and it is not the way I operate. The reason I show people how to do things badly is because that is the way I have lived my own life. I have never fastened on one thing and gone after it. Instead, I have tried this and that, delighting in experimentation and failure."

He paused, as if looking back over a very long period of time. "Along the way, I have had the most fun when I was engaged in this process with other people. Teaming with them. Reaching out through them, encouraging them, falling short and rising along with them."

I knew that Finnegan often channeled his advice and applied it in particular fields, so I wasn't sure if he was speaking specifically or generally.

"In all settings?" I cut in. "Or is this simply something you have done in business, or in social or personal-growth endeavors?"

"In all settings. In all settings," Finnegan responded, continuing to gaze at the ceiling, but now clutching his lapels as if to hang on to the idea. "We are human beings in all settings. And in all times and places, we do best when we operate in harmony with those around us. That means helping them to do badly, showing them that we are doing badly ourselves, and giving them faith that we all will muddle through."

"You mean each of us should be an inspiration to others?"

"Of course!" said Finnegan. "An inspiration, a beacon, a teacher. All around us, there are people who are terrified of failing, who feel badly about doing badly, who get frozen up at the very idea. When they see that we are willing to do things badly, to fall on our faces, to chuckle and get up and go on, they too will be willing to do things badly. To go through the shadowed valley that leads to the bright light. They will accept themselves, they will accept us, they will accept life and all its flaws."

For a few moments, I fell silent. I had never before taken this view of Finnegan's Way. I had seen it as a practical way of overcoming difficulties, an effective method for getting from Point A to Point B, of evading personal-behavior traps, but nothing more.

I had not considered its wider implications, or the idea that it was a way of moving forward through life in concert with the people around me.

Still, I was reluctant to show Finnegan how impressed I was. I did not want to give up my role as his questioner, his skeptic, the analyst of his thoughts and ideas. Something told me this would not be good for me or good for him.

I needed knowledge, and he needed a foil, a sounding board to use as he refined his techniques and contemplated their implications.

Besides, I did not want our sessions to end, and I sensed that totally accepting his ideas would mean that we would have no more discussions. Because of this, I returned to my original query.

"So," I said. "What do you get out of this?"

Finnegan laughed and shook his head. But now he seemed entirely comfortable with the question. And he appeared entirely comfortable with me.

I sensed that my analysis had been correct. He seemed especially pleased to see that our roles had not changed, that our back-and-forth would continue. He thought for a moment, looked around him, and settled on an answer.

"What do I get out of this?" he asked. "Why, a cup of coffee." He inclined his head. "Will you have one with me?"

CHAPTER 7

Imperfection Creates Partners

"YOU ARE REALLY AN INSPIRATION," I said to Finnegan, after we had downed our latest jolts of caffeine.

As usual, his dose of coffee had the high color rising on his cheeks and his eyes flashing. He was primed for more discussion, and I knew he was ready to take on a challenge.

"Here's the thing, however," I continued. "I'm not clear about how we should help others do things badly."

"*How* makes a big difference, so you are right to ask," said Finnegan, rubbing his hands together vigorously as if preparing to take on a physical task. "There is a particular technique that seems to work like magic, and I'll be happy to explain it to you."

I was excited at the prospect of more useful knowledge, but my growing curiosity about Finnegan himself overcame me.

"Did you develop this technique yourself, or did someone teach you?" I asked. "As often as we talk, I never discover much about your history. In fact, I've never heard a thing about you up to this point. You seem to have labored in obscurity."

Finnegan chuckled—rhythmically, like a well-tuned motor at idle.

"I suppose I have, at least in your terms," he said. "But obscurity is not such a bad place in which to labor. It is quiet and restful. The English, you know, have a peculiar fondness for obscurity, a fascination for life lived out of the public eye."

"Are you English, then?" I asked.

"It is interesting that you should ask that," Finnegan replied.

Then he was off on a completely different tack, and I never learned the truth. In fact, it took me a while to work him back around to our original subject, that of how to help someone perform badly.

"Oh yes, that," he said, finally. "I learned the basics from a fencing instructor."

Finally, a little personal information!

"I didn't know that you knew fencing."

"There again," replied Finnegan. "At any rate, I was performing particularly poorly one day—this was in a shabby but world-famous fencing school in the outer precincts of Paris—and a veteran instructor said to me, 'Don't worry about it. Worrying is not your job.'

"'Not my job?'" I shot back. "'How am I supposed to improve if I don't worry about my performance?'"

"'Because that is *my* job,'" he said. "'Your job is to

38

make mistakes. My job is to help you overcome them.'

"Suddenly, a weight was lifted from my shoulders. I didn't have to worry about everything. I had a partner in my struggle, and I could do as badly as I wanted without being concerned about it. Instead of having my mind clouded with guilt over my miscues, of having to fight through psychological barriers as well as physical challenges, I was free to concentrate on the relatively minor problems of what I was doing wrong with my feet and hands."

Finnegan, it seemed to me, had developed into a master of instruction himself, as well as an excellent advisor. His latest tale got me thinking about workers at my publishing company. Some spent so much time apologizing about screw-ups that their minds never turned to the task at hand.

I began to see how crippling misdirected energy could be.

"Is this technique good for dealing with employees who spend all their time worrying?" I asked.

"It is, indeed," said Finnegan. "Especially for those who are always trying to make their work flawless. It is a good thing to point out to them that perfection can, in fact, be a bad thing. Beware when the boss tells you that your proposal is perfect or 'the best she's ever seen.' That usually means it is doomed. If a proposal is perfect, it leaves no room for other people to get involved and exercise their creativity. This frustrates them, and no matter how good the proposal or the pitch really is, they will find a way to scuttle it. The goal in pitching an idea is to make it very good, but not perfect. Give everyone a chance to make it better."

"So imperfection creates partners, is that right?" I said.

Finnegan chuckled throatily and slapped me on the shoulder. "You are getting better at this than I am," he said.

"And does that principle apply in areas other than business?"

"It certainly does," said Finnegan. "The technique we just discussed—taking on the task of worrying about the mistakes of others—is quite effective in working with teenagers. Obviously, there are many worries in this area. Teenagers must always deal with a great deal of psychic turmoil before they can settle down and do what needs to be done."

I was thinking of a friend's teenagers. They certainly had been difficult, and I knew she would welcome some good advice on how to get along with them, if I could induce Finnegan to explain his technique in more detail.

"Exactly how should you approach them?" I asked.

"Just as I said," replied Finnegan. "When you deal with a teenager, don't tell her she's a horrible person because she misbehaved. Instead, tell her it's her job to misbehave, and it's your job to see that she doesn't misbehave. This way, she sees clearly that you understand youth is a period in which people try new things, doing some things right and other things wrong. She also sees what being an adult is all about. Taking responsibility, helping other people, setting a standard for behavior."

He paused, nodding vigorously to make his point. I sensed that this was a technique he felt strongly about—one he had spent much time developing.

"This is a lot better than putting all the responsibility on an often-confused young person. She really doesn't know the right way to act, though she pretends she does. But she does know instinctively that it is right for her to experiment and test limits."

He spread his hands, as if laying out the spectrum of teenage behavior in front of my eyes.

"Keep in mind that often the reason she acts badly is to assert her independence. Good! She must become her own person, and she knows this. Instead of struggling to make her just like you, which she will never agree to— if she has any backbone—make it clear that you understand she is different from you and that she *should* be different. You can't imagine how comforting it is for a teenager to be told this."

I absorbed this fascinating piece of advice, but I was also still seeking for clues about Finnegan.

"You speak as if you have had teenagers of your own," I said.

He grinned. "I do speak that way, don't I?" he said. "Good for me! It is very comforting of me to do that."

"In fact, have you had teenagers?"

He coughed a bit and looked down at the table. His lips moved wryly as if he were making a decision. Perhaps our relationship had developed to a significant point. Was I about to experience a revelation?

"I have told you about my fencing instructor, and now you want me to tell you whether I have had teen-agers," Finnegan said at last, with his usual attitude of casual good humor. "One by one, you are wresting all my secrets from me, and soon I will no longer be able to luxuriate in the obscurity that I find so restful."

I snatched at this admission. "But only the English have a fondness for obscurity," I said. "You told me that yourself. That means you must be English."

"Did I say *only* the English?" asked Finnegan. "How careless I am getting."

CHAPTER 8

Do Many
Things Badly,
All At Once

I HAD BEEN SPENDING SO MUCH time with Finnegan that I had been neglecting my business. At least, I thought I had. However, when I went into the office one day, I found things humming along pretty well.

Everybody seemed to be in a good mood, and they were plugging away at their jobs—or, in some cases, at new tasks they were tackling.

The staff writer who had taken a shot at the problem of the pages falling out of our books was quite enthusiastic.

I found her desk buried in books about printing processes and glue. She'd been thinking through all sorts of approaches, she said, moving as quickly as possible. And she had begun to isolate the difficulty.

The sales people were doing a brisk business. One of them, I saw, regularly shifted his pitch in midstream—

when one selling point didn't work, he'd move speedily to another. And he was obviously enjoying himself, and transmitting that enjoyment to his customers.

Overall, I noticed a great deal of activity, of hustling, of creative ferment in the office. The energy of the place seemed to have been boosted.

I wanted to get back to Finnegan for his analysis.

But when I next approached him at his table, he was occupied with another client. This was a middle-aged man whose face and posture sagged, and whose clothes exhibited signs of sloppiness—an absent button, an unpressed collar, a belt that had missed a loop.

He struck me as a very low-energy person, so I was surprised to hear Finnegan laying down a rapid-fire series of items for him to attend to.

The man left, and I brought this up with Finnegan.

"I believe you are changing your style," I told him. "You have always seemed so philosophical, but you were firing orders at that man like a gymnastics coach. What, exactly, was going on?"

"So you thought my approach was different, did you?" he asked. "Perhaps it was, slightly. But my advice in this instance was a very minor variation of what I have been propounding all along. It's true that I may have stepped up my own energy level in an attempt to boost the electricity in this man's brain, but that was merely an attempt to inspire him by example."

"So, once again, you were advising him to do things badly?"

"Of course," Finnegan replied. "You do not need many principles in my world."

I crowded closer to the table. "Still," I said, "I am very interested in the variation in this instance. It seems to me that small changes in style can make a big difference in terms of accomplishment, that the way you approach a task is key to how well you do it."

Instead of responding verbally, Finnegan jumped from his chair, clicked his heels together, and began to perform an Irish jig. His legs pumped vigorously, his hands slapped in rhythm, and his head nodded in time.

The other customers laughed and cheered as he flung his arms outward and spun about, amazingly graceful. Then, his face glowing with perspiration, he dropped back into his chair.

As always, I was trying to figure him out.

"So," I said. "Does that mean you agree with me?"

"Exactly," said Finnegan, blotting his forehead with a white linen handkerchief. "We were talking about style, so I felt it might be best to demonstrate its importance, rather than just talking about it."

"And you were demonstrating something else," I replied.

"Really?" rejoined Finnegan. "And what might that have been?"

"Energy," I said. "High energy."

"You are so good!" Finnegan joked gently, as he tucked away his handkerchief. "And why was I doing that?"

I thumbed my chin. "Well, I believe it had to do with the advice you gave that rather dragged-down looking man. You were trying to raise his energy level. You believed that would be crucial in turning his life around."

"Correct."

"But how?"

"A simple, powerful technique," Finnegan replied.

"Which is?"

"To do lots of things badly, *all at once*." Finnegan paused. "The way to jump-start yourself is to leap right in and try lots of things without thinking about them too much. If you are having trouble making friends, smile at everyone you see, and follow up quickly if you get a response. If you are looking for a job, make lots of calls, do lots of interviews, rush around like a madman. If you take too long with projects, start several of them and as soon as one begins to bore you, shift quickly to another. Life is movement, and moving gets things accomplished."

"That's what's happening at my company!" I said, excitedly.

"Really?" said Finnegan. "You must have told your workers the story of the amateur salesman."

"No," I said, shaking my head. "They are acting instinctively, based on my original advice. I've never heard the story of the amateur salesman."

Finnegan grinned. "Well, you are going to hear it now, just in case you run into some workers who need an illustration of how the technique works."

46

He settled back and started in:

"Back when such an occupation was much more common, a young man took a job selling sets of encyclopedias door-to-door. On his first day, a wise old salesman briefed him and his fellow new salesmen. A reasonable success rate, he told them, would be selling one set of encyclopedias a day. With that, he sent them out into the neighborhoods.

"At the end of the day, they reassembled and the old salesman asked them what they had done.

"The man two seats to the left of the young man spoke up. 'I sold two sets of encyclopedias in my first ten stops and knocked off for the day,' he said. The old salesman nodded.

"Then, bubbling with pride, the man just to the left of the young man reported, 'I sold *four* sets of encyclopedias in my first fifteen stops, then I settled back for the rest of the day and went over the strategies that had helped me be so successful!' The old salesman nodded.

"It was the young man's turn. He hung his head and said disconsolately, 'I knocked on one hundred doors, not even stopping for lunch, and didn't make a single sale. Sorry.'"

"Again, the wise old salesman nodded. For a few moments, he seemed to be thinking. Then, suddenly, he pointed at the first two salesmen and said, 'You will never succeed in this line, and you might as well quit right now.'

"He turned to the young man. 'You, on the other hand, will be a fine salesman. The key, as you fig-ured out, is to knock on many doors. And to keep on knocking.'"

Finnegan paused and leaned back, leaving me to voice the moral of the story.

"Do many things badly, all at once," I said. "And keep doing them."

CHAPTER 9

Take Care, But Not Too Carefully

I ALWAYS ENJOYED A MUFFIN or two when I had my discussions with Finnegan. I was partial to zucchini muffins, but every now and then, I was also tempted by the chocolate-chip variety. There was something to be said for apple-cinnamon, too.

"I certainly admire a man who wears his weight well," Finnegan said to me one day. "Some men would be upset if they were bulking up as much as you are, but I detect that you see a certain virtue in exercising all the holes in your belt."

It was hard for me to reply to him just when he said this, because I had my mouth full. But I came right back as soon as I swallowed.

"So you're saying I'm getting fat."

Finnegan waggled a finger at me.

"You are so blunt!" he said. "You must learn subtle ways of expressing yourself, as I have. However, since you raise the issue, it is true that my formerly slim companion has expanded rather frighteningly. How much weight have you put on since we met. Ten pounds, twenty?"

"Who's keeping track?" I shot back. "I prefer to monitor my weight badly. And I would think that would fit right in with your program."

Finnegan was greatly amused.

"Now, now. You are becoming my equal at witty back-and-forth, and I cannot have that. I must re-assert my moral authority. Remember: We do things badly only as a means toward doing them well, not as an excuse for sinking into poor physical or psychological shape."

I pushed back my plate of muffins, one of them half-eaten. But Finnegan, seeing the stress of unsatisfied hunger in my eyes, pushed them back to me.

"Eat, eat," he said. "Surely you don't think I am going to counsel you to quit eating 'cold turkey,' as you Americans say so vividly."

Happily, I resumed my breakfast. "I was certainly hoping you wouldn't," I said. "But you had me worried for a moment."

Finnegan made a good-natured gesture of dismissal.

"Oh, heaven forbid that I should worry anyone," he said. "Didn't I tell you that I am the one who does the worrying for those under my care?"

"You did tell me that," I said, sweeping some crumbs from my shirt and reaching for another muffin. "So now you are going to tell me that you will worry about my diet and I don't have to?"

Finnegan sipped his coffee. "That's true," he said. "But that is not the technique for getting you on a healthy diet. To do that, you are going to practice the Distraction Method."

I leaned back with a sigh of satisfaction. There's nothing like a few muffins in your stomach to get you in the mood for dieting. You feel relaxed, full, and ready to take on anything.

"All right," I said. "I'm wide open to being distracted. How are you going to do it?"

Finnegan sighed with exasperation. "As you should know by now, I am not going to do anything. *You* are going to do it. Helped, of course, by my invaluable guidance."

"Well, guide, guide!" I said. "But first, why don't you tell me why my own dieting efforts haven't worked up to this point. I have tried various diets, but none seem to work."

Finnegan spread his hands on the table as if he were spreading open a book.

"Yes, here are the various diets you have tried. Let's see: *The One-Egg-A-Day Diet, The Abominable Snowman Diet, The Beverly Hills Real Estate Saleswoman With the Funny Hat Diet.* Am I right? There's a new one every week. I often think they should dispense with the nonsense, write one huge diet book and call it *The Best-Selling Diet-Author's Diet: The Last Diet You—And the Author—Will Ever Need.*"

"Very funny," I said. "And your point is?"

"Simply this," said Finnegan. "These diets all require you to get enthused about some special regimen—odd foods, or weird combinations of starches and protein and whatever. Now, a world-class dieter could follow these odd and demanding instructions. But an ordinary human finds them mind-numbingly hard."

"I'm sorry," I said, "but you don't understand the dynamics. People like these diets because they offer hope of a breakthrough. Therefore, they get people's emotions involved. Dieters get excited, and that enthusiasm helps carry them along, even though the regimens are hard."

Finnegan was shaking his head. "The enthusiasm carries them for a while, but it inevitably fades. What people really need is a diet they don't have to pay attention to."

"You mean they need to diet badly?"

"Not exactly," said Finnegan. "Though you can put it that way if it helps keep the idea fixed in mind. They simply need to take care, but not too carefully."

Finnegan was always coming at ideas in an interesting way, but sometimes he could be too subtle. Fortunately, he usually was thinking of a practical principle.

"You mentioned the Distraction Method," I said. "Is that the key to effective dieting?"

"Yes, it is," replied Finnegan. "I'm pleased that our intervening discussion did not distract you from the main point."

"Oh, come on," I said. "You are becoming too fond of word play. Tell me how the Distraction Method works."

"Very well," he said. "It is simplicity itself. And it relies on the fact that our culture is so concerned with dieting that all of us know which foods are good for us without consulting any book at all, faddish or not. Lots of fruit and vegetables, cereals, fish—that sort of thing. You are probably more up on this than I am. The challenge is to get these foods into our bodies in place of things that aren't so good—sweets, red meat, and so on."

"And we do that by—?"

"By getting the bad foods out of our refrigerators and cupboards, and filling them up with the good foods. Then by distracting ourselves when we are eating."

Finnegan took my empty muffin plate and set it aside, then resumed.

"Much of our problem with food is that we concentrate on it too much. When we sit down to eat, we focus on the food, and if we are dieting, we focus on the idea that we aren't getting enough of the foods we crave. Better, then, to eat healthful food while we are doing something else—reading, watching television, working—and are focused on something other than food. If we eat enough when we are distracted, we will be far less likely to be hungry in those moments when nothing occupies our attention."

"I get it," I said. "We must eat *only* when we are distracted."

Finnegan gave me a look of exasperation.

"Now, is that realistic?" he asked. "Remember the principle of doing well by doing badly: few people can stick to a regimen. We must try our best to eat only when distracted until the habit of eating well begins to form. But we must not be so harsh with ourselves that the occasional lapse throws us into despair."

I felt abashed. "Can I propose another approach, then?"

"Of course."

"Take care, but not too carefully."

Finnegan grinned.

"Now you are getting somewhere."

CHAPTER 10

Seek Relationships— It's Not a Bad Thing

I THOUGHT OF FINNEGAN ONLY as a counselor. That view was so strong that I never expected him to have any other relationship with people.

But one day, just as I entered the shop, I noticed a quite attractive woman leaving his table, slightly flushed, as if she had just told him something intimate.

As I pulled up my chair and arranged my coffee and water cups on the polished surface, I noticed that he, too, was glowing with a warmth even beyond his usual good temper.

I took my time before speaking, sipping carefully as I watched him over the rim of the cup. Finally, I sighed and put the cup down.

"Well, Finnegan," I said. "You seem to have made a conquest."

"How do you deduce that?"

"That lovely lady was blushing, and since I doubt you would ever say anything out of the way to a woman, I'm sure that she was doing so because she was interested in you."

"Do you think so?" said Finnegan, with absolute innocence. "Well, one must be open to all possibilities. Romance is one of the great rewards of life."

I reached for a spoon and stirred my coffee, though I wasn't actually mixing anything into it. For a while, I had used sugar, but now I contented myself with stirring. The action distracted me from the fact that I wasn't adding calories.

"I suppose so," I said. "Though it is so difficult these days for me to fit romance into my schedule."

Finnegan seemed to draw back.

"Is it now?" he said. "My view is always that romance should infuse one's schedule—the romance of creativity, of endeavor, and, yes, the romance of relationships. Living life to the fullest must include love. But, strangely enough, these days many leave it out of the equation."

"Don't get me wrong," I said. "I'd really like to find a woman to share my life. But it's just hard to find the right one."

Finnegan was looking very grave, as if I had presented him with a complex mathematical equation which was going to take some time to work out.

"Dear me," he said. "'The Right One.' Yes, I can see how it might be difficult to find that one. Who knows, for instance, if she is anywhere near us as we speak? She could be in Louisiana, or in Rangoon, or

Yemen. Perhaps we are even in the wrong century. She could have lived during the Age of Enlightenment and passed from the world forever. Or perhaps she will not be born for another hundred years."

I was dumfounded.

"What are you babbling about?" I said.

"I am merely saying that you speak of The Right One as if there is only one, and if you don't find her you will just have to do without."

Finnegan could be so pig-headed. True, he was right much of the time, but he was so pig-headed.

"That's not what I'm saying at all," I protested. "It's just that the women I go out with aren't appropriate. If one is intelligent, she's not very good-looking. If one likes the kind of music I like, she drives me crazy by not showing up on time. If one is both intelligent and good-looking, she's into her career so much that she doesn't pay enough attention to me."

Finnegan was listening to all this very seriously. "And how do you deal with all these 'inappropriate' women?"

I hope I didn't sound testy, but I reacted immediately: "Why, I drop them. One date, and then I'm off. Why waste time on them?"

"Why, indeed?" replied Finnegan. "It is obvious that you are a quality man when it comes to relationships. Nothing but the best."

He was looking at me in a certain way, and I knew what was coming.

"Oh, no," I said. "Surely you aren't going to tell me to date badly and keep on doing it. That's crazy."

"Is it?" said Finnegan. "Then why did you come up with it on your own?" He cocked his head. "Surely not through my poor influence during all these weeks of trying to improve your life?"

"But this is different," I said. "I can't apply principles that are successful in the workplace to my relationships with women. My personal life is just so much more. . .personal."

"You may be right," said Finnegan. "But let's examine the situation and see if you are. When we talk about helping people in the workplace by permitting them to do badly, what are we doing?"

"Well," I said. "I guess we are giving them a chance."

"And what are we doing when we free them up from our rigid expectations of what they are or should be?"

I thought about it. "We are allowing them to be who they really are and make the most out of it. Humanity beats conformity."

"And what happens when we trust them and give them a chance?"

"We are allowing them to be creative and to have fun, to get excited about what they are doing."

Finnegan took a drink of coffee and looked around him at the various customers inside the shop and those he could see through the windows. They presented quite a variety.

"I don't know about you," he said, "but the women

I enjoy are those who feel free to show me who they really are, who are creative and involved in life, who are able to get excited about me and about everyone and everything else around them." He looked upward speculatively and nodded to himself. "It is quite amazing how many women are like that. Of course, they don't always show it. Not if men are measuring them against a yardstick of supposed perfection."

"Hmmm," I said. "Like a boss that won't give his workers a chance."

"Yes," said Finnegan. "Just like that."

He reached into his lap, and removed a Panama hat that I hadn't noticed when I first came in. Its appearance surprised me. I had never seen him wear a hat. But he seemed quite comfortable with it. He settled it on his head, tilting the brim with a deft hand.

"I'm sorry to leave you so abruptly," he said with a wink. "But I have a date for lunch."

CHAPTER 11

Life is Struggle, but Struggle is Life

I HAD NEVER ASKED FINNEGAN about the little book that he carried, and he never mentioned it. But I was sure it was not just some novel or biography, or a travelogue that he particularly enjoyed.

In time, I came to suspect it must be a compilation of his own or some other person's wisdom. I particularly believed so when his discussions took a philosophical turn.

One November day, when the coffee shop and the tables out in the sun were busy with winter visitors, I noticed him reading with special intensity.

Right then, I decided I would delve more deeply into his commitment to doing things badly.

When I approached, the book disappeared into his pocket, as it always did.

But as we settled into our usual conversation, I purposely asked sweeping questions, hoping to draw him into revealing the underpinnings of his mode of thought, or to induce him to mention something he had gotten from this book.

"I've never asked you why your methods work," I said, shifting my coffee cup this way and that and not looking at him, because I felt I might be moving into unwelcome territory. "I mean, there must be hidden principles that cause them to be so effective."

When he responded, his voice was as cheery as ever.

"I've been wondering why you haven't asked," he said. "With your inquiring mind, you must be eager for that sort of information. And it *is* valuable."

I looked up, saw his usual genial expression, and hurried to assure him.

"It's not that I'm prying. You have been so generous with me and others. I don't want to presume to demand your deepest secrets."

His smile seemed just for me. I felt a profound sense of companionship, and I was grateful.

"My deepest secrets, indeed," Finnegan said. "Well, my deepest secret is that I have no secrets. The principles of my methods are open for all to see. The world around us shows us their worth every day."

I was a bit put off by this. In fact, I thought he was trying to be evasive, though I felt guilty for thinking so.

"How can that be?" I asked. "I wasn't aware of them until you told me. And I still need your guidance to refine and practice your techniques."

"You are a good friend," he told me warmly. "But you are giving me far too much credit. I am not a touchstone of wisdom, revealing arcane knowledge. The value of doing things badly is obvious. Only those who get bogged down in the details of life cannot see it. If you believe one mediocre performance defines a person, you are bogging yourself down. If you see doing badly as part of a process that in time will lead to good things, you have gained understanding."

"Then a failure to understand is simply a failure to look?"

"Yes, certainly," replied Finnegan. "Arthur Conan Doyle, the famed author of the Sherlock Holmes stories, said that all women are beautiful. What did he mean by that? That there is beauty in the essence of being a woman. That there is beauty not only in the physical nature of women, but in the way they approach life, their reactions to it, what they give back to it.

"Sherlock Holmes once chided his friend Watson, saying, 'You see, but you do not *perceive.*' This is a failure of many people. It is not that they don't see beauty, but that they do not look for it. To find beauty, you must look into the nature of people. If you look keenly enough, you will find it."

I was absorbing all this, picking my way carefully.

"Then you are saying that people fall short in their efforts to gain happiness because they are poor observers of the world around them?"

Finnegan put up a hand. "Not only that. They fall short also because they do not *engage* that world."

"You mean that they spend too much time on the sidelines?"

"Some spend *all* their time on the sidelines," he replied. "In a world bombarded with media, many let the world happen to them rather than going out after it."

"Are you saying they are not working hard enough for success?"

"They are not working hard enough for anything," said Finnegan. "*Success*, after all, is not the pinnacle of life. Especially since, to many, it means only financial success. We sometimes say that someone who has achieved financial success has 'arrived.' What does that expression mean, anyway? Where could you possible *arrive* in this world that you would want to stay and never leave? Who ever really makes enough money, or attracts enough love, or gains enough power? No, the aim must simply be to keep moving forward in life. If you were never to 'succeed' but kept moving forward toward your goals, you would have an enormously enjoyable life."

At this point, Finnegan unconsciously placed his hand on the coat pocket that held his book.

"Look at the basketball player, Michael Jordan," he said. "The best basketball player in the history of the world. In mid-career, he decided to play professional baseball! Now, he certainly intended to play baseball well, but he must have known he would never play it as well as he played basketball. And, in fact, he was a mediocre baseball player, at least by his standards. But what a challenge! Once again, as he had when he first learned basketball, he experienced the thrill of improving little by little, of struggling, of being engaged! This is the mark of someone who is not afraid, who understands the glory of the struggle itself."

"So *that* is the basic principle," I said.

"Yes!" said Finnegan. "Life is struggle, but struggle is life. Happiness, as near as we can approach it in this world, is simply getting up each day and doing *something*. Badly, well, or some other way. Feeling the blood pulsing in your veins and arteries, brushing the sweat from your brow, hearing the cogs in your brain clicking and whirring. Being in the fight. Slapping your companions on the back, thrusting your fist in the air, giving a hell of a cheer. And then enjoying a wonderful laugh."

At this, he jumped upright, both his fists shooting upward.

"Don't spend your life on the couch!" he exclaimed. "Get out there and do things badly! You'll never regret it."

CHAPTER 12

Where's Finnegan?

THE FOLLOWING DAY I WENT to the Starbucks and Finnegan wasn't there. I didn't think much about it. He sometimes skipped mornings, and I didn't have anything pressing to ask him. I would see him the next day, or the next. There was no real hurry.

The fact was, I had run out of things to ask him. He'd already given me advice that applied to every part of my life. I got my coffee and went out into the winter sunlight. Settling down, I made an accounting of all he had done for me.

My fitness had improved. I was doing ten bad push-ups and ten bad sit-ups a day, and it was so easy. I knew I'd fallen into a habit that would be hard to break, so I was considering doubling the number of repetitions. Why not? It would be better for me. But I was definitely not going to push myself. I wasn't going to get to the point where I was thinking too much about what I was doing. Why bother, when I could do so much good for myself by exercising badly?

Same thing with my diet. I kept fruit and fresh vegetables around, but I made a point of munching on them when I was watching TV and my thoughts were otherwise occupied. Unconsciously, I was putting away a lot of good stuff, so much so that sometimes when I considered an ice-cream sundae, I just wasn't hungry for it. When I really *wanted* that sundae, of course, I had it. Otherwise, I would have been risking eating too well, and I certainly didn't want to do *that*. I'd done so well eating badly (relatively speaking), that I didn't want to risk flipping over to a hard-nosed regimen I knew I couldn't follow.

My business was booming. The woman staff writer handling the binding problem had taken care of that issue, and she and my other employees had never seemed happier. Given the option of working badly, they were doing incredibly well.

My romantic life had improved, too. Since I had started dating badly, I'd noticed something. Many of those women I thought weren't pretty enough or fashionable enough or successful enough were terrific company. Instead of putting every woman I saw on a personal yardstick, I just went with my instincts.

If there was *anything* about a woman I liked—her smile, the deft way she handled a work situation, her interest in a particular kind of book or movie—I'd ask her out for coffee. And if that worked out halfway well, I'd ask her to dinner. I made a lot of wonderful friends, and began dating one of them steadily, a woman I never would have considered in the past.

When I finally realized that no woman was perfect, I began to see little perfections in all of them.

As I left the coffee shop that day, I was excited. I was brimming over with gratitude to Finnegan, and I was eager to see him so I could tell him.

I made a point of hitting the Starbucks every day, hoping to catch him. Each day, I'd approach the glass door with anticipation, already peering through the bright sun-glow, hoping to catch sight of him at his corner table. But each day as I entered, I'd glance toward the corner, and the table would be empty.

After a couple of days, I began asking the coffee server if he had seen Finnegan. The first day I asked, the coffee server was the same one who had originally pointed out Finnegan to me. He just shook his head. Then he shrugged and smiled, as if Finnegan's absence didn't matter all that much.

The next day that server was gone and he never appeared again. When I asked the replacement servers about Finnegan, and even when I asked about the previous coffee server, they seemed not to know what I was talking about.

I was mystified. But I kept going to the shop on the off chance that I'd see Finnegan. I made it every day for two straight weeks and he wasn't there.

But on the fourteenth day, when I looked at his table, I realized a very strange thing. *No-one* had been at that table for two weeks. The whole shop was crowded, and it had been almost this crowded every day, but no-one had used that table.

That day, after I ordered my double espresso, I went and sat at the table myself. I felt like relaxing and, in truth, I had time to relax. Things were going very well at work. I wouldn't be needed there for several hours, perhaps not for the whole morning.

I sat there sipping my coffee, taking care not to spill any of it on my white linen suit, or on the mahogany polish of my cap-toed shoes. After a while, the newest coffee server passed the table on his way outside to sweep the sidewalk, and he smiled and nodded at me, as if he was very glad I was there.

I was glad I was there, too. This was quite a friendly place, and the warmth coming through the windows was comfortable. In a way, it was as if Finnegan were still here. After a while, I removed a slim volume from my pocket, a volume bound in rich cloth, and began to read it.

I was thoroughly enjoying myself when a troubled-looking man approached me. There was something wrong in his life, I could tell. He nodded at me, then at the coffee server, and said, "Sorry to disturb you, but the man over there said you could give me some good advice."

I smiled at him and slipped the slim volume into my pocket, making no particular effort to hide its title.

I waved toward the chair across from me.

"I'll certainly try," I said. "Though I'm afraid I might do it badly."

He settled down, looking relieved.
"From what I hear, that will be just fine," he replied.
And it was.

Charles Kelly doesn't look much like Finnegan, does he? Or perhaps you think he does. In any case, you can write to him at pulpnoir22@aol.com. Or visit his website, hardboiledjournalist.com. He'll tell you the basis for many of his stories about Finnegan.

PRAISE FOR FINNEGAN'S WAY

"This short and sweet little fable has an amazing amount of comforting wisdom in it. I've struggled with the fallout from not meeting perfectionistic standards my whole life. This amazing book shows why that approach fails, and how giving myself and others the permission to do things badly works. There are a lot of books out there now about self-compassion, but this little book sums it all up perfectly, as far as I'm concerned, and it's really entertaining and easy to read, too. I'm so grateful that I discovered it."—Nettie McClain, Vancouver, WA.

"This isn't the usual motivational book that tells you how to be perfect in all ways. Quite the contrary. Finnegan, who appears to be perfect, advises the opposite. He tells us that better results can be had by avoiding perfection, and that taking the wrong path can eventually lead to the right path...*Finnegan's Way* offers realistic and guilt-free methods to self-improvement. I highly recommend it."—Paul Perry, *New York Times* bestselling author of *Closer to the Light*.

"For frustrated perfectionists everywhere, *Finnegan's Way* offers a simple solution to finally quiet the self-critical voice in your head and release you from your paralyzing fear of failure: do what you do badly and enthusiastically…As I've incorporated the ideas in the book, I feel liberated; it put the fun back into my work."—Laura D. Lloyd, Houston, TX.

"What a refreshing little book! Self-help at its finest; light and humorous. Several unique ways of living our lives more satisfactorially. I highly recommend this book; it is a keeper to be read again and again."—Sandi Wallace, Amazon reviewer.

"Don't let the subtitle fool you: the secret power of doing things badly isn't for slackers. It's about giving yourself, and those around you, the freedom to release the potential we all seem to repress one way or another…There is, of course, no ultimate roadmap to success and happiness, but there's nothing like an insightful, modern-day fable to help nudge you in the right direction. What I found almost immediately, while reading the introduction, was a pleasantly infectious voice that carried over to the main text and continued to hold my interest to the last page. I couldn't read it fast enough, anxious to see how the story would end, and I wasn't disappointed. I can't imagine anyone finishing *Finnegan's Way* without a smile on their face."—John Schmierer, author of *Ocean Boulevard* and *Gravedigger's Moon*.